IMAGES
of America

THE BERKSHIRES
COACH INNS TO COTTAGES

D1613617

THE ENTRANCE HALL, 1891 QUEEN ANNE. I am indebted to my mother for an early and enduring interest in houses. She considered driving from one "Open House" sign to another to "see inside"—a great Saturday outing appropriate for all ages. My early interest ripened when I restored this house. Tearing it down to the bones and restoring it to the last finial gave me an appreciation for the craftsmanship, even artistry, of architecture. (Author's collection; photograph by Paul Rocheleau.)

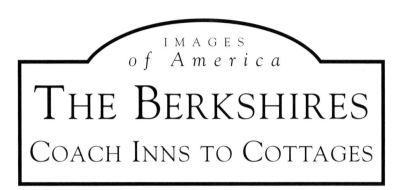

IMAGES
of America

THE BERKSHIRES
COACH INNS TO COTTAGES

Carole Owens

ARCADIA

First published 2004

Published by Arcadia Publishing,
Charleston SC, Chicago IL, Portsmouth NH, San Francisco CA

Printed in Great Britain

Library of Congress Catalog Card Number: 2004107294

For all general information, contact Arcadia Publishing:
Telephone 843-853-2070
Fax 843-853-0044
E-mail sales@arcadiapublishing.com
For customer service and orders:
Toll-free 1-888-313-2665

Visit us on the Internet at www.arcadiapublishing.com

To my mother (1923–2003), who loved houses and made homes.

THE LIBRARY, 1891 QUEEN ANNE. My interest broadened to social history when I wrote *The Berkshire Cottages*. A house like this was meant as testimony to the social standing of the owner. There were abundant natural resources and an uninterrupted flow of cheap and skilled labor. Every artistic detail, like the carefully designed and hand-wrought brick chimney piece, attested to the taste and consequence of the inmates. (Author's collection; photograph by Paul Rocheleau.)

4

CONTENTS

ACKNOWLEDGMENTS

All historians are indebted to those who wrote before them. History is a thoughtful version of children's blocks. Each writer lays a new block, which is dependent upon the blocks beneath. The historian interested in the Berkshires is fortunate. The foundation blocks have been carefully and continuously laid by residents interested in recording their roots and preserving their historic places. I have relied upon the following who preceded me: J. E. A. Smith, *History of Pittsfield 1734 to 1800*, town of Pittsfield (1868), and *History of Pittsfield 1800 to 1876*, town of Pittsfield (1876); Clark W. Bryan, *The Book of Berkshire*, Clark W. Bryan & Company (1887); E. A. Morley, *Lenox 1886*; Charles F. Warner, editor, *Picturesque Berkshires*, W. F. Adams Company (1898); *Open House in New England 1937*; Natalie Sedgwick Colby, *Remembering*, Little, Brown & Company (1938); Sarah Cabot Sedgwick and Christina Sedgwick, *Marquand, Stockbridge: 1739 to 1939*; Ellery Sedgwick, *The Happy Profession*, Little, Brown & Company (1946); Olive Colton, *Lenox* (manuscript *c.* 1950); William R. R. Brooks, *Williamstown: The First Two Hundred Years*, McClelland Press (1953); David Wood, *Lenox: Massachusetts Shire Town*, town of Stockbridge (1969); Carole Owens, *The Berkshire Cottages*, Cottage Press (1984); Carole Owens, *Bellefontaine*, Canyon Ranch (1988); Mary V. Flynn, editor, *The Stockbridge Story*, town of Stockbridge (1989); Lion Miles, *New England Quarterly*, March 1994 and June 1996; newspapers the *Berkshire Courier*, *Lenox Life*, and the *Valley Gleaner* collectively 1850 to 1902; and state of Massachusetts survey maps *c.* 1750, *c.* 1800, 1855, 1876, and 1904.

Photographic collections from the following institutions helped make this book possible: the Library of Congress Manuscript Division, the Frederick Law Olmsted National Historic Site, the Providence Library Reference Department, the Berkshire Athenaeum Local History Room, and the Williamstown House of History. Thanks go to Norma Probst at the Cranwell Resort; Peter Hopkins at the Crane Archives; Georgia Massucco at the Lee Library; Pam Torres and Gretchen Fairfield at the Red Lion Inn; Linda Hall at the Williams College Archives and Special Collections; James Miller at the Sheffield Historical Society; Will Garrison with the trustees of Reservation; Barbara Allen at the Stockbridge Library Historical Collection; Dennis Lesieur, director of the Lenox Library; and Amy LaFabe, Lenox Library reference librarian.

The author is also grateful to the following individuals generous enough to share their time, expertise, and photographs: Maggie Lidz, Robert and Dr. Ruth Markovitz, Hoagy Carmichael, and George Crocker. Special thanks go to my own good Samaritan, landscape architect Tom Elmore; writer, editor, and all-around good guy Nick Noyes; Maureen Johnson Hickey, art historian and curator of A Return to Arcadia, Berkshire Museum, 1990; Lion Miles, writer and gifted researcher; Christopher Baumann for unstinting aid; and Ed Darrin, who has preserved and protected an exceptional document collection and is always knowledgeable and generous.

INTRODUCTION

For those who have visited the Berkshire Hills, the natural beauty is evident, but the richness of the history may come as a surprise. This small and charming part of New England was not settled until 100 years after the pilgrims landed on Plymouth Rock. Once settled, however, the Berkshire villages rapidly gained in importance disproportionate to their size. At the turning of almost any page in American history, the Berkshires receives at least honorable mention.

In the 18th century, the villages were home to missionaries, those who fought the Revolution, and those who attended the Continental Congress. In the early 19th century, the Berkshires was home to the writers and educators who shaped the voice of the new nation, and the painters who captured its image. In the late 19th century, the businessmen and politicians who guided the nation from agriculture to industry, from a fledgling nation to a powerful one, had homes in the Berkshires. In religion, business, law, science, and the arts, the region has attracted the best and the brightest. Thoreau, Hawthorne, Melville, Aaron Burr, Daniel Webster, Oliver Wendell Holmes, Bret Hart, John Jacob Astor, Harriet Beecher Stowe, George Inness, Thomas Cole, Edith Wharton, Henry James, Mark Twain, Vanderbilt, Biddle, Morgan, Whitney, Roosevelt, Cleveland, and more have been visitors besotted by the natural beauty and drawn to one another.

"Come tell me how you live."—Lewis Carroll.

Our buildings are the repositories of our memories. Houses are the keys to the soul of a culture. To understand how people live is to understand their economics, politics, and mores. To understand how one person lives is to understand his social standing. *The Berkshires: Coach Inns to Cottages* shows where visitors lived when in the Berkshires. By simply seeing and describing the dwelling places, each of the three historic periods are better understood.

Early Americans came to the Berkshires in stagecoaches, on horseback, or on shanks' mare (on foot). For $1.75, one could travel from Stockbridge to Hudson, but it took 5 hours; Hartford to Albany took 15. Travel was slow and arduous. The first visitors sought inns in order to break the journey, eat, rest, refresh, and change horses.

In the mid-1800s, the railroad came to the Berkshires. Hissing, puffing, brakes screeching, the railroad cut across the landscape and forever changed it. It brought people in larger numbers and at a faster pace. The notion of traveling for pleasure was born. Railroad hotels were built beside the coach inns. A new economic base was established in the region. From their beginnings as farmers and mill workers, Berkshirites became innkeepers to the outlanders.

The American Lake District was a period in Berkshire history when painters, writers, clergy, and educators built the first summer houses. They came with the warm breezes and left when they felt the first cold snap in the autumnal air. Locals called that time of year "apple blossom to apple drop." The literati returned every year, earning the title of "permanent summer residents." They celebrated the beauty of the region in prose, poetry, and paint. In this way, the reputation of the Berkshires was established.

The Gilded Age resort was formed in the late 1800s when the nation's princes of commerce and barons of banking discovered the Berkshires. The hills were punctuated with the great estates that Cleveland Amory called "the wings and turrets of outrageous fortune." The names of the owners still conjure visions of wealth and grandeur.

All these sojourners left a mark upon the Massachusetts landscape; their lives left a mark on the arts, literature, politics, and economics of the entire country. In word and picture, find out who they were and how they lived.

THE DINING ROOM, 1891 QUEEN ANNE. Ironically, those intent upon creating lush and elaborate surroundings also attempted certain economies. The front stairs were broad and sweeping. The servant's stair was narrow and plain. More expensive woods, detailed carving, and decorative ceilings were reserved for formal rooms. A single door that connected the butler's pantry to the dining room was clad in mahogany, with sterling silver pulls on the dining room side and oak with brass pulls on the pantry side. (Author's collection; photograph by Paul Rocheleau.)

One

EARLY AMERICAN

COACH INNS AND RAILROAD HOTELS

THE STEPHEN VAN RENSSELAER HOUSE. A propitious combination of wealth and location facilitated the movement of building materials and workmen to this site along the river in 1765. The Berkshires was inland, and the settlers less August; therefore, 18th-century Berkshire architecture was simpler. This house was enlarged in 1820 and remodeled by architect Richard Upjohn in 1843. Later, it was disassembled and rebuilt on the Williams College campus. (Courtesy of the Williams College Archives and Special Collections; illustration by Currier and Ives.)

THE MISSION HOUSE, 1739. The General Court of Boston authorized a mission to "civilize and Christianize" the Housatunnuck Indians in 1736. On Thanksgiving Day 1739, missionary John Sergeant stood before his congregation with true thankfulness. He had traveled from Yale College to Stockbridge, built his meetinghouse (church) upon the plain, found a wife (Abigail Williams), and completed a new home. Moreover, on June 22, Stockbridge became an incorporated town. (Courtesy of the Red Lion Inn.)

THE MISSION HOUSE MUSEUM TODAY. The Mission House was built on the hill among the white settlers, away from the Native Americans and the meetinghouse. Mabel Choate, 200 years later, sought to restore the oldest house in Stockbridge. She was advised to move it off the hill, away from the eroding winds, to the plain where the meetinghouse and Native-American settlement once stood. Today, the location of the Mission House is symbolic of John Sergeant's close relationship with the Housatunnuck Indians. (Courtesy of the trustees of Reservation.)

THE JONATHAN EDWARDS HOUSE, 1751. John Sergeant died in 1749. In 1751, missionary Jonathan Edwards arrived. He purchased a house from a Native American, improved it, and was the first white man to live on the plain. In this house, he wrote two important religious works. Oddly, the one entitled *Freedom of the Will* argues that man is utterly dependent for all action upon God. Having just proved that all actions originated with God, Edwards had some difficulty completing his second work, *Original Sin*; he prevailed at last by explaining that original sin was not an action of God, but a proof of His absence. Edwards's daughter Esther married Aaron Burr, the president of Yale College, and gave birth to the future vice president of the United States, also named Aaron Burr. The grandfather was hailed as a man of serenity and logic, while the grandson was plotting to establish in New England a separate northern confederacy, and when exposed by Alexander Hamilton, Burr shot Hamilton. (Courtesy of Lion Miles.)

A YARD IN STOCKBRIDGE. An unidentified child sits near the kitchen garden, surrounded by chickens. The area around the settlements was untamed. It was necessary that a household be self-sustaining. The six original white settlers of Stockbridge—John Sergeant, Ephraim Williams, Josiah Jones, Timothy Woodbridge, Joseph Woodbridge, and Ephraim Brown—were each granted 400 acres to allow for the accouterment of early properties: barn, animal yard, kitchen garden, and acreage suitable for cultivation. (Courtesy of the Red Lion Inn.)

THE CALLENDER COACH INN. Sheffield was established by legislative act in 1733 with one condition attached. The "proprietors" of the town had to make a "good and feasible" road at their own cost and labor. *Good* and *feasible* were relative terms. If the trees were marked and the pass one cart in width, this was acceptable. Roads of the 18th century were not as fine as the one that ran in front of the Callender Inn, shown in this early-19th-century photograph. (Courtesy of the Sheffield Historical Society, Mark Dewey Research Center.)

A REGULATION HOUSE. In 1750, the General Court of Boston laid out 63 lots of 10 or 12 acres each in Hoosac (Williamstown). On horseback, in carts, on foot, through woods, over muddy tracks and rock outcrops, settlers went to Williamstown. In exchange for a lot, prospective owners had to clear a minimum of five acres and build a house that met the regulations of the General Court of Boston, "a regulation house." (Courtesy of the Williamstown House of History.)

A REGULATION HOUSE INTERIOR. The houses were to be 18 feet by 15 feet, clad with split shingles. This provided a one-room house with a chimney on one wall. The fireplace was the source of food, light, and warmth. The house, intended for a family of two, could be enlarged by adding another 18- by 15-foot section, creating two rooms, a fireplace in each. (Courtesy of the Williamstown House of History.)

A REGULATION HOUSE EXTERIOR. By 1753, the population of Hoosac was 25 in 13 regulation houses. (Courtesy of the Williamstown House of History.)

A HARTFORD COURANT ADVERTISEMENT, SEPTEMBER 13, 1837. "Safe pleasant and expeditious traveling Through by daylight Leave the United States Hotel at 4 o'clock a.m. (Sundays excepted) and arrive in Albany at $7^{1}/_{2}$ p.m. The coaches are new strong and easy in motion, and every care has been taken to procure careful obliging and steady drivers." Travel from Hartford to Albany took 15.5 hours. A place to stop, rest, and change horses was mandatory. (Courtesy of the Historic Merrell Inn.)

THE 1783 HOUSE. Located at the nexus of New York, Massachusetts, and Connecticut, stage and post roads crisscrossed the county and spurred growth. The stages stopped at Berkshire inns, but some inns only served the fares and refused to serve the drivers. Perfectly located and built in the coach era, this house may not have been an inn, but it is still important as the future home of illustrator Norman Rockwell. (Courtesy of Betsy Holtzinger.)

THE HART FAMILY PICNIC AT THE RED BIRD INN. After dropping the fares at one inn, the coachmen repaired to the Red Bird Inn for their victuals. In the cradle of democracy rocked many a sign that read "Coachmen positively declined." Capt. Solomon Hart was a blacksmith as well as an innkeeper and welcomed coachmen and horses alike. (Courtesy of the Red Bird Inn; photograph by E. R. Sisson.)

THE MERRELL INN. Coach inns were of varying quality. In an effort to ensure uniformity, or at least decency, licenses were required. For example, the following was issued on August 29, 1749, at the Springfield Courthouse: "License is granted to Josiah Jones of Stockbridge to be an innkeeper, taverner, and common victualer in said town the year ensuing for selling strong liquors by retail and he recognizes what sureties as ye law directs for his keeping good rule and order in his house." (Courtesy of the Historic Merrell Inn.)

THE MERRELL INN INTERIOR. The Merrell was an inn of quality and, like most coach inns, was originally a private home with a stable and large meeting and dance hall. The "keeping room" is the English term for the family's general sitting room, where they ate and worked. A more appealing, if less accurate, meaning is a room designed for "keeping the family together." (Courtesy of the Historic Merrell Inn.)

THE RED LION INN. In 1775, Silas and Anna Bingham moved to Stockbridge to open a store. Soon, they added an inn and tavern. When Bingham died in 1781, his widow became the first female innkeeper in the Berkshires. She sold the inn to Silas Pepoon, who promptly went bankrupt; the inn sold for $12 at auction. It has burned and been rebuilt, renovated, and renamed, but for two centuries, a "large and elegant house" has provided lodging, a good meal, and a store on the same corner in Stockbridge. (Courtesy of the Red Lion Inn.)

MAIN STREET, STOCKBRIDGE. Most coach inns served the locals as well as the outlanders. A coach inn was a place to buy a drink, eat a meal, and socialize. Some had ballrooms the length of the second floor. Locals could buy a newspaper and, after 1829, collect the mail. Here, men lounge on the porch of the Red Lion Inn. (Courtesy of the Red Lion Inn.)

MAIN STREET, STOCKBRIDGE. Church and town governance were indistinguishable. Vestrymen built roads, and laws regulated moral conduct. When the minister's sermons or lifestyle did not please the congregation, it was the town that cut his salary. The minister's salary was paid by the barter system and, since it consisted of essentials like food and firewood, cuts were a harsh penalty. In 1761, landlord David Root was found guilty and fined as he "did willingly and willfully suffer and permit singing, fiddling, and dancing in his dwelling place there being a tavern." In 1779, Lavinia (Mrs. John) Fisk was excommunicated because her husband was constantly heard to swear in public. *She* was punished for marrying him in spite of his swearing; *he* was not excommunicated because he was not a church member. Townsfolk stood between the church and the inn, between sanctity and temptation. (Courtesy of the Red Lion Inn.)

THE FIRST "COURTHOUSE INN." From 1787 to 1867, Lenox was the Berkshire shire town (county seat). The tiny rural community became a destination for lawyers, judges, and other learned folk. The first courthouse was built in 1792 just up the road from this inn that served "those who had business with the court." (Courtesy of Ed Darrin.)

LENOX, 1839. "Moving house" was a literal term in the Berkshires. New Englanders saved string and old newspapers for alternative uses; they were not apt to raze a house. In 1815, the new courthouse was built and this corner became prime real estate. In 1829, the Berkshire Coffee House meant to profit by it. The old inn was moved. Shown on right side of the road are the new courthouse, the Berkshire Coffee House, and town hall. (Author's collection.)

THE BERKSHIRE COFFEE HOUSE. In 1853, William Curtis moved from Stockbridge to Lenox and purchased the Berkshire Coffee House. Members of the Curtis family had been Stockbridge selectmen and tax assessors. The family owned so many mills and tanneries that a section of Stockbridge was called Curtis Mill and then Curtisville. Still, William Curtis made an intelligent move. Long after the mills and tanneries closed, the hotel thrived. It still stands in Lenox today. (Courtesy of the Lee Library; photograph by E. A. Morley.)

THE FIRST PITTSFIELD TRAIN DEPOT. "Monday June 15, 1825, a great day! General Lafayette visits Pittsfield."—*Pittsfield Sun.* Lafayette left Albany on horseback at 6:00 a.m. He arrived in Lebanon Springs at 2:30 p.m. and changed to a coach. At 6:00 p.m., he arrived at the Merrick Coffee House, next to the Bullfinch church. The trip was a little over 40 miles and had taken 12 hours. In 1842, the train from Albany to Pittsfield, traveling on average 25 miles per hour, arrived in less than 2 hours. (Courtesy of the Berkshire Athenaeum, Kennedy Collection.)

THE BERKSHIRE HOTEL. Pittsfield was incorporated in 1761, the same year Hampshire County was divided, creating Berkshire County. Pittsfield folk joined the ranks of Berkshire innkeepers and became old hands at hospitality, but they were also known for their political furor. In 1808, at the Berkshire Hotel, the two passions clashed. The owner was a Federalist. During Jefferson's presidency, he became so incensed with the Democrat-Republicans that he swore never to serve them. When a party of Democrats arrived, he was thrown into turmoil. His honor was at stake: he had been heard swearing to refuse service. Yet, he was a respected Berkshire innkeeper and could not turn away honest custom. He fought and resolved his inner conflict: the Democrats were allowed to collect their own food and were forced out the door to eat in the orchard. (Courtesy of the Berkshire Athenaeum, Kennedy Collection.)

THE IRVING HOUSE. Built of brick and situated to catch the summer breezes, this inn catered to visitors who arrived by train. Dalton was on the Northampton–Albany stagecoach line until 1842. By 1847, it was on the Albany–Boston railroad line. Both journey and destination were described as enjoyable. The views from the train, as it chugged through mountains and beside the Housatonic River, "are beautiful in the highest degree." (Courtesy of the Crane Archives.)

A HARPER'S ILLUSTRATION. Stagecoach travel fought for survival against the iron horse and lost. Train travel was faster and more comfortable. Travelers could plan to go farther, and time on the train was anticipated as part of the vacation. The stagecoach became obsolete. If the coach inns wanted to survive, they had to "gussy up" to compete with the new train hotels. Otherwise, they were razed or restored to their origins as private homes. (Author's collection.)

THE RED LION INN. Old coach inns refurbished to greet their new customers. The Red Lion added a fresh coat of paint and a decorative white railing around the porch. (Courtesy of the Red Lion Inn.)

THE RED LION INN DINING ROOM. The dining room sported new wallpaper, a very modern touch. The large windows made the room sunny and bright, and the tables were covered in white linen, set and ready for the guests. (Courtesy of the Red Lion Inn.)

THE RED LION INN. Shown are the contents of a lady's traveling case: stays, corset, and slippers; mop cap and "bit o' lace"; collars and boots; and, of course, hat, fan, and dress. Then as now, women's fashion changed: in 1840, the dress included a wide scoop or V neck, back fastening, and tight sleeves; in 1850, a high neckline, standing collar, and flared sleeves; in 1860, a high neckline, front-buttoning bodice, and white undersleeve; in 1870, a pointed white collar, a trimmed bodice, and bell-shaped sleeves. (Courtesy of the Red Lion.)

A SAND SPRINGS ADVERTISEMENT. Sand Springs, trumpets Dr. Lloyd's brochure, had curative powers. In fact, no other medication was necessary; Sand Springs waters cured gallstones, acne, bellyache, headache, and eczema. One only needed to know whether to drink it, soak in it, or wash with it, and sleeplessness would vanish and soft, glowing skin would appear. All this was accomplished by the power of the water alone: "no soap should be used with Sand Springs water. (Courtesy of the Williamstown House of History.)

THE HOTEL AT SAND SPRINGS . Early in the 17th century, Native Americans varied their route so they could break their journey at Sand Springs to rest and drink the magic waters. Therefore, Sand Springs was the first spa in Berkshire County. In 1800, an entrepreneur built a log cabin beside Sand Springs. Whatever his master plan for further development, nothing materialized. Sand Springs bubbled, the cabin stood, and not much else happened until 1805. That year, S. Lewis Lloyd, M.D., built the hotel at Sand Springs. (Courtesy of the Williamstown House of History.)

THE SECOND HOTEL AT SAND SPRINGS. The original hotel burned to the ground in 1886. A new, if slightly less regal, hotel was built. The spa flourished for 60 years. (Courtesy of the Williamstown House of History.)

HEATON HALL. Heaton Hall boasted a grand lobby, ballroom, music room, reading room, dining hall, and observation tower looking out over the valley and distant hills. Upstairs, Theodore Roosevelt was among the dignified guests. Downstairs, Ida Mall came from Brooklyn and joined the staff. In the basement, village children arrived at the kitchen door in the late afternoon to help staff shell peas for dinner in exchange for a dish of ice cream. (Courtesy of the Library of Congress.)

THE OAK LAWN HOUSE. Even before the train came to town, eight coaches a day—four in each direction—made regular stops in Stockbridge. When the train replaced the stagecoach, what had been a steady stream of visitors became a flood. Seemingly, no number of inns and hotels was too many. The Oak Lawn House was located along the north–south highway in Stockbridge. (Author's collection.)

THE MAPLEWOOD. In 1812, the Maplewood was commandeered for barracks and officers' quarters. It was described as three buildings, each three stories high and 130 feet long with piazzas. In 1822, it was used by the Berkshire Medical College and, later, as the Maplewood Young Ladies Institute. At no time did anyone comment favorably on the architecture but always noted that the grounds were exceptionally beautiful. Finally, the Maplewood was remodeled as an inn. (Author's collection.)

THE GREYLOCK. "The Greylock will be conducted with especial reference to the comfort and convenience of its guests, no pains being spared to make the house worthy of the patronage of the summer visitors." This promise by the management would have been for naught without the delicate sentence buried near the end of the brochure: "The sanitary arrangements and system of drainage [for all 100 rooms] are complete." (Courtesy of the Williams College Archives and Special Collections.)

THE GREYLOCK STABLES. Railroad hotels like the Greylock went far beyond the simple comfort of coach inns. They provided luxuries like a "bowling alley in the annex, a billiard room, dancing nightly in the ballroom." As at any coach inn, there was accommodation for coaches and horses, but their function was not the same. "A good livery and boarding stable connected with the hotel. Stages meet every train." (Courtesy of the Williams College Archives and Special Collections.)

THE ASPINWALL. The Aspinwall stood on a higher hill and spread longer and wider than any other. It purported to offer a higher quality of absolutely everything. It was "the last word" in Berkshire hotels. Unfortunately, the phrase was unwittingly prophetic. The Aspinwall failed and indeed became the last of the large railroad hotels built in the Berkshires. (Author's collection.)

THE STOCKBRIDGE TRAIN STATION. The train carried passengers across the continent, while the coach was reduced to ferrying them the short distance from station to hotel. (Courtesy of the Stockbridge Library Historical Collection.)

THE ELM STREET MARKET. The horse and carriage, still a familiar sight, was reduced to the short haul. Here, Stockbridge shopkeepers prepare to make local deliveries. (Courtesy of the Stockbridge Library Historical Collection.)

TOM CAREY'S RIG. This small horse and buggy picked up packages and mail from the train station and delivered them to houses and hotels. It also served as the local taxi. (Courtesy of the Stockbridge Library Historical Collection.)

Two

THE AMERICAN
LAKE DISTRICT

SUMMER HOMES

THE ASPINWALL HOTEL. William Aspinwall was one of the founders of the Century Association. Begun in 1847, its purpose was "advancing American art and literature by establishing a library and gallery of art and by such other means as shall be expedient and proper." Of the 100 founders, many were associated with the Berkshires. (Author's collection; photograph by the Detroit Publishing Company.)

THE VAN RENSSELAER MANSION, C. 1840. Thomas Cole's work laid the foundation for the Hudson River School, according to *Return to Arcadia*. Cole first traveled through the Berkshires on the Albany Northampton Road in 1833. The following year, at his studio at 1 Wall Street, New York, he showed the Berkshire painting *View of Hoosac Mountain and Pontoosuc Lake near Pittsfield*. (Courtesy of the Williams College Archives and Special Collections; oil by Thomas Cole.)

NATURE'S WORK OF ART. Frederic Edwin Church, student of Thomas Cole and a Century Association founder, spent the summer of 1847 in the Berkshires as the guest of Cyrus West Field. Inspired, Church painted at least eight Berkshire views, including *View from Stockbridge*. The area was becoming the artist's haunt and home. Cyrus Field bought the painting, and his brother David Dudley Field bought the land. They were two of the "Fabulous Fields." (Photograph by the author.)

THE OFFICE OF JONATHAN EDWARDS FIELD. In 1858, the first transatlantic cable was sent from London, not to Washington or New York or even Albany, but to this unassuming law office in Stockbridge. Cyrus Field, who laid the cable, was "phoning home." He told the local lawyer, his brother, "Cable successfully laid. All's well." Children were let out of school, church bells were rung, and guns were fired into the air as Stockbridge celebrated. (Photograph by the author.)

THE HOME OF JONATHAN AND STEPHEN FIELD. Jonathan Field's son Stephen sent the first reply cable, "On earth peace and good will toward men." Stephen Field invented the electric trolley car, which he ran on a circular track in his front yard to the delight of Stockbridge children. When a streetcar company wanted to run a commercial line through town, Stephen Field led the fight against it. A good Stockbridge resident first and inventor second, he resisted change to his beautiful village. (Photograph by the author.)

LAUREL COTTAGE. Frederic Church possibly stayed here, at the home of Cyrus Field's brother David Dudley Field in 1847, but certainly Herman Melville and Nathaniel Hawthorne met here at lunch three years later. Literary historians mark the day of August 5, 1850, because Melville attributes his ability to write *Moby Dick* to having met Hawthorne, and thus dedicates the book: "To Nathaniel Hawthorne in token of my admiration of his genius." (Courtesy of the Red Lion Inn.)

EDEN HILL. Three of the Fabulous Fields were lawyers—Stephen Johnson Field, named to the Supreme Court by Pres. Abraham Lincoln in 1863, Jonathan Field, and David Dudley Field. In 1855, David Dudley Field bought Sergeant's Hill, where John and Abigail had built the Mission House in 1739, and in 1870, built his summer house, Eden Hill. Ironically, David Field codified New York penal law and represented Jay Gould, Jim Fisk, and Boss Tweed. (Courtesy of the Red Lion Inn.)

THE HENRY MARTYN FIELD HOUSE. Rev. Henry Field's connection to the arts is unique. He married a woman about whom books were written and movies made. Henriette Deluzy-Desporte was governess to a French noble family. When the husband murdered his wife, authorities suspected he had done it for love of the family governess. From the intrigue of the French court to a quiet hill in Stockbridge, the journey of Henriette Deluzy-Desporte is recorded in Rachel Field's *All This and Heaven Too*; in the movie, Bette Davis played Henriette. (Courtesy of the Red Lion Inn.)

SEDGWICK HOUSE, 1785. The Fabulous Fields were not the first or only Stockbridge residents to lure "the best minds" to the Berkshires. Of her father, Catharine Sedgwick wrote, "When there were no steamers, no railroads, and a stage but once a week, Gentlemen made their way to Stockbridge [to see him]." Guests included Aaron Burr, John Van Buren, Washington Irving, Oliver Wendell Holmes, William Cullen Bryant, and Daniel Webster. The conversation was "natty and jaunty and gay." (Author's collection; drawing by Harry Fenn.)

Sedgwick House Today. Theodore Sedgwick's daughter Catharine was a well-known author of romances and moral tales. Her fame continued to attract people like Henry Wadsworth Longfellow and Harriet Beecher Stowe to Sedgwick House. Famed actress and author Fanny Kemble wrote, "Of the society that gathered summer after summer in the pleasant hills, Miss Sedgwick was the center and the soul." A member of the Sedgwick family has occupied this house for 220 years. (Photograph by the author.)

The William Cullen Bryant House. Bryant practiced law in Great Barrington. After the Sedgwicks convinced him to go to New York and write, he became a Century Association founder. Many credit him, pen in hand, with encouraging the next great influx of artists to the Berkshires. "There is no tonic," he wrote, "like the Housatonic." (Courtesy of the trustees of Reservation.)

BONNIE BRAE. The Ivison-Parsons family gathers on the lawn of Bonnie Brae. During the Depression, Catherine Parsons was forced to sell the house. In the 1960s, J. Graham Parsons retired from foreign service and returned to Stockbridge. Bonnie Brae came on the market at just the right moment, and the former ambassador to Laos and Sweden was able to buy his childhood home. With a brief interruption, Bonnie Brae remained in the family for 124 years. (Courtesy of J. Graham Parsons.)

LINWOOD. Charles E. Butler purchased 50 acres and built Linwood in 1859. He was a partner in the New York law firm of Butler, Southmayd, and Choate. Both his partners constructed summer homes in Stockbridge, and the youngest, Joseph Hodges Choate, built directly across the valley. Butler liked to say he could keep an eye on his junior partner from his front stoop. (Author's collection.)

Broad Meadows. This house stood solidly on a foundation of hotel money. Eramus Curtis (of the Curtis Hotel) and Daniel B. Fenn (manager of the Red Lion Inn) were early owners. Fenn sold it to Irene Botsford, daughter of Henry Botsford, founder of the Chicago meat-packing business. Irene and Bernard Hoffman were married at Broad Meadows. The Hoffmans donated to Stockbridge one of its most artistic treasures—the Botanical Gardens. (Courtesy of Thaxter P. Spencer.)

A Literary Triumvirate. By temperament and family ties, these noted writers were attached to the Berkshires. Melville wrote *Moby Dick* at Arrowhead while looking out his window at a "humpback hill." Emerson's daughter Ellen attended Miss Sedgwick's School; his sister Susan married G. G. Haven's brother William. Thoreau spent a night on Mount Greylock, and while he said the advertisements in the local paper were better written than the columns, he seemed inspired by the Berkshire Hills. (Author's collection.)

NAUMKEAG. Founder Joseph Hodges Choate said the Century Association had "the most charming circle of men. We youngsters sat at their feet in devout admiration." That circle included Berkshirites Sam Ward and Ogden Haggerty. Accompanied by patron Ogden Haggerty and a guest of Sam Ward, George Inness walked a Berkshire road, painting *Storm Clouds* (1847) and *Hills of Berkshire* (1848). Choate built Naumkeag on the same road 40 years later. (Courtesy of the Providence Library.)

THE LENOX COURTHOUSE. The stretch between the Lenox Courthouse, the Berkshire Coffee House, and the post office was called "the Whirl-About." Rushing back and forth from a court session to a meal break were judges pontificating and lawyers hailing clients, complainants and those complained against. Coachmen bellowed, whips cracked, and horses snorted, as all those who had business with the court were drawn to Lenox along "the great road" from Albany to Boston. (Courtesy of the Lee Library; photograph by E. A. Morley.)

A LENOX STREET SCENE. The inn was filled to capacity when court was in session. The Lenox Academy for Boys drew the sons of the finest families; naturally, parents visited them. The village's reputation spread, and Lenox grew in importance disproportionate to its size. In 1857, the guest list at the Curtis Hotel included Bret Hart, John Jacob Astor, James Russell Lowell, Chester Arthur, and the British prime minister. (Courtesy of the Lenox Library.)

THE OLD ROAD FROM STOCKBRIDGE TO LENOX. In 1821, Charles and Elizabeth Sedgwick traveled along this road from Stockbridge to establish a Lenox household. The price of land had risen from 30 shillings ($3.60) per 100 acres prior to the Revolutionary War to $50 for a single acre, as the intelligentsia was attracted to Lenox. In 1828, the Sedgwicks opened Miss Sedgwick's School for Young Ladies on Walker Street. Their sister Catharine soon joined them, a literary salon in her wake. (Author's collection.)

REV. JUSTIN FIELD'S HOUSE. Young ladies who attended Miss Sedgwick's included Charlotte Cushman (a future actress "better known than President Polk"), Alice Delano, Ellen Emerson, and the granddaughter of Pres. Martin Van Buren. Jennie Jerome, later Lady Randolph Churchill, mother of Winston, boarded in this house on Courthouse Hill while a student. Her slate was found in the attic with "JJ" carved into the wood. (Photograph by the author.)

MISS LIPPICOTT'S SCHOOL. Next-door on Courthouse Hill, this house was identified as a school. It may have been, but it likely also served as a boardinghouse for students attending Miss Sedgwick's or the Lenox Academy for Boys. According to the school, "[Lenox Academy] boys are not lodged in dormitories, but are given homes in good families where they are under the direct charge of good Christian men and women." (Courtesy of Ed Darrin.)

HIGHWOOD, 1845. At Highwood, Sam Ward entertained Jenny Lind, Fanny Kemble, Margaret Fuller, George Inness, Nathaniel Hawthorne, and Catharine Sedgwick, but on this day, he was waiting for the chimney man. "December 16, 1845, Richard, In a new house, at this season of the year, after sparing no pains or expense, to be unable to use half my house for the smoke and fear of fire because the mason is too great a man to keep his appointments, is very vexatious."—Letter to Richard Upjohn, friend, architect, and president of the American Institute of Architects, 1857–1876. (Courtesy of the Lee Library; photograph by E. A. Morley.)

THE LITTLE RED HOUSE. On August 6, 1849, Anna Ward wrote in her diary, "Passed the morning in driving about trying to look up a house for the Hawthornes." No mention is made of how far afield she drove, but the house found for Nathaniel Hawthorne was literally on her doorstep. Hawthorne took up residency in June 1850 and called his new home the Little Red Shanty. (Author's collection.)

A VIEW OF STOCKBRIDGE BOWL. While at the Little Red Shanty (1850–1852), Hawthorne wrote *The Scarlet Letter* and *The Wonder Book*. He named the parts of this view, seen from his window, Shadowbrook, Tangle Wood, and Bald Summit. Two years earlier, staying across the road at Highwood, George Inness had been inspired by the same view and painted the four- by six-foot oil *Hills of Berkshire*. The Berkshires was America's Lake District, the haunt and inspiration of artists and writers. (Courtesy of Ed Darrin.)

HIGHWOOD TODAY. From 1845 to 1850, Anna Ward recorded opinions of her guests at Highwood. "Mrs. Butler [Fanny Kemble] possesses a fine voice and quick intelligence, but I would not like to discourse with her." "Hawthorne has a face full of feeling and is painfully shy." "Jenny Lind, the best music I ever heard . . . but she has trouble over money affairs with [P. T.] Barnum." "George [Inness] has a sad soul." In 1850, the Wards left Highwood. (Photograph by the author.)

FAIRLAWN, 1837. The little colony at Lenox was attracting artists and patrons, but it was also a family affair. Elizabeth Kneeland (Mrs. Ogden) Haggerty of Ventfort and Charles Kneeland of Fairlawn were siblings. Charles and Elizabeth Sedgwick were also near relations. Highwood was let to William Aspinwall and Caroline Sturgis Tappan. Annie Haggerty Shaw's mother-in-law was a Sturgis, and Sunny Bank was owned by her sister-in-law. (Courtesy of the Lee Library; photograph by E. A. Morley.)

VENTFORT. Ogden Haggerty was in residence at Ventfort in 1852 when this letter was sent from George Inness to Sam Ward: "Three shillings is all I possess and know not where to get more. I dread asking Mr. Haggerty as I have been almost entirely supported by him since I have been back from Europe." Actually, Haggerty had paid for the European tour, too, as Inness's patron. Paintings by Inness decorated the walls of Ventfort. Haggerty's daughter Annie married Robert Gould Shaw, colonel of the first African American regiment in the Civil War, the Massachusetts 54th. The couple honeymooned at Ventfort. From the battlefield in 1863, Shaw wrote to his wife, "I keep that country place of ours before my eyes." Shaw was killed. Annie Shaw never remarried, and after the death of her parents, she made it a condition of sale that Ventfort never be torn down. (Courtesy of the Lee Library; photograph by E. A. Morley.)

SUNNY BANK, 1865. Annie Haggerty Shaw's sister-in-law Ellie Shaw married Gen. Francis C. Barlow. Annie's marriage had lasted 77 days; Ellie was the luckier, as her husband survived, and after the war, they built Sunny Bank. Legend states that long after Ventfort was sold, just before her death, Annie returned. She knocked on the door of Ventfort, and asked to sleep once more in her honeymoon bedroom. The wish was granted. (Courtesy of the Lee Library; photograph by E. A. Morley.)

THE PIERREPONT SUMMER HOME, 1870. Edwards Pierrepont lived here. His unusual first name reflects his relationship to both Jonathan and Sarah Pierrepont Edwards. Pres. Abraham Lincoln appointed Pierrepont a special prosecutor in his administration. After Lincoln's assassination, Pierrepont prosecuted co-conspirator John Suratt. Pres. Ulysses S. Grant then named him U.S. attorney general. Accused of being lax in prosecuting infractions of the law during Reconstruction, Pierrepont was blamed for its failure. (Courtesy of the Lee Library; photograph by E. A. Morley.)

ETHELWYN, 1875. Built by H. M. Braem, this home was later purchased by Mrs. Robert Winthrop. As part of the Massachusetts Bay Colony, the Winthrops were considered founders of Massachusetts. They are also credited with bringing the fork to the New World. Mrs. Winthrop's son Grenville joined the Lenox Colony when he purchased the Elms. (Courtesy of the Lee Library; photograph by E. A. Morley.)

THE ELMS, 1858. Originally owned by William Ellery Sedgwick, this house was enlarged and renamed Groton Place by Grenville Winthrop. It is not documented if his ancestors actually brought the fork to Plymouth, but they certainly did bring the civility symbolized by the use of utensils rather than fingers at meals. With the grand vistas before him, Winthrop raised two daughters. They in turn married the help—a local chicken man and the chauffeur. (Courtesy of the Lee Library; photograph by E. A. Morley.)

THE PERCH. Fanny Kemble established her reputation as a fine actress in England before arriving in Lenox in 1836. She purchased this house on a hill and busied herself reading Shakespeare at Miss Sedgwick's School and at private literary gatherings at Sedgwick House and Highwood, charming Henry Wadsworth Longfellow, William Cullen Bryant, and Nathaniel Hawthorne. Kemble left Lenox to marry Pierce Mease Butler of Georgia. (Courtesy of the Lee Library; photograph by E. A. Morley.)

FANNY KEMBLE. Fanny Kemble married a Georgia plantation and slave owner. Nonetheless, she wrote a strong condemnation of slavery. Not surprisingly, the marriage failed, and she returned to Lenox. There, she charmed a young man named Robert Gould Shaw. The man who would one day be colonel of the Massachusetts 54th and die leading his African American regiment into battle had been very impressed with Kemble's views on equality and probably a little in love with her. (Author's collection; drawing by Thomas Lawrence.)

CATHARINE SEDGWICK. Although her books are no longer widely read, Catharine Sedgwick at one time was "the most popular author in the United States" (the *London Times*). Many admired and sought her in the Berkshires, as they had her father before her. One woman who came, along with her brother Rev. Henry Ward Beecher, was Harriet Beecher Stowe. She spoke of abolition, saying, "The Union will have to give way." Catharine Sedgwick called her "Obstinate Harriet." (Author's collection; drawn by Harry Fenn.)

BLOSSOM FARM, 1865. In his day, Rev. Henry Ward Beecher was better known than his sister. His sermons were reputed to be a combination of St. Paul and P. T. Barnum. He lived in a modest farmhouse upon a hill, where he wrote *The Star Papers*. A proponent of Social Darwinism, Beecher wed survival of the fittest to church doctrine and proclaimed the wealthy were God's favorites; the poor were sinners. (Author's collection.)

THE BURTON HARRISON HOUSE. Novelist Constance Cary Harrison, her home pictured here, participated in fund-raising for the pedestal of the Statue of Liberty. Although the statue was a gift from France, the pedestal was to be paid for by the American people. She planned an art exhibit as a fund-raiser, intending to include a "literary portfolio" with samples of writing by well-known authors. She asked her friend Emma Lazarus to contribute a poem. A few days later, Harrison received the poem; it began, "Give me your tired your poor your huddled masses yearning to breathe free." The portfolio sold for $1,500, and the original poem disappeared. (Courtesy of the Lee Library; photograph by E. A. Morley.)

PLUMSTED COTTAGE. Built by Alfred Devereux, this cottage was later sold to Joseph Whistler. Joseph's uncle George Washington Whistler was an engineer and bridge builder. George's second wife, Anna Mathilda McNeil Whistler, gave birth to son James Abbot in 1834. While her husband traveled as far as Russia building bridges, Anna Whistler "sat to" a painting—*Whistler's Mother*—and wrote a cookbook. Joseph's brother Ross also bought a house in Lenox. (Courtesy of the Lee Library; photograph by E. A. Morley.)

ALLEN WINDEN, 1882. When J. P. Morgan was asked where he might build a summer house, he replied, "Near my friends Morris K. Jesup and Charles Lanier." Morgan did not build in Lenox, but he was a good friend to Lanier. Having invested heavily in a railroad only to learn he owned the train but not the tracks, Lanier almost crumbled. Morgan "helped him out of his troubles." (Courtesy of the Lee Library; photograph by E. A. Morley.)

BELVOIR TERRACE, 1886. Morris K. Jesup left school at age 12 and went to work. He became a successful railroad banker and member of the board of J. S. Morgan & Company. Jesup, along with J. P. Morgan, served as a trustee of the Metropolitan Opera and the Museum of Natural History. (Author's collection.)

OAKSWOOD, 1878. Sam G. Ward, returning to the Berkshires, asked architect Charles Folsom McKim to design a house. Comparing Highwood and Oakswood, one could sense the change that was taking place in Lenox. In the art colony, the entertainment was conversation and reading aloud from the classics. Ladies wore muslin dresses "run up" at home, and Highwood was a fine house. Lenox was being discovered by society, which would work quite a change. (Courtesy of the Lee Library; photograph by E. A. Morley.)

YOKUN, 1794. Lenox was called Yokunville prior to incorporation in 1767. The name was changed to honor Charles Lennox, the third duke of Richmond, because he said, "I wish from the bottom of my heart that the Americans may resist and get the better of the forces sent against them." This house was named to recall earlier days. (Courtesy of the Lee Library; photograph by E. A. Morley)

YOKUN REMODELED. The American Lake District was a community of comfortable but unostentatious homes. Richard Goodman's house, as shown in the previous photograph, was in keeping with the homes of his neighbors. In the 1880s, however, a prescient Richard Goodman engaged architect Charles Folsom McKim to redesign, enlarge, and improve Yokun. (Courtesy of the Library of Congress.)

A BERKSHIRE PICNIC. Prior to the Civil War, a desire was born out of combined religious reform and nationalism to perfect the United States, to improve life. It was considered the role of societies and churches to carry forward these reforms. As a God of Love replaced the Puritan God of Retribution, there followed a commitment to causes like abolition, suffrage, world peace, and the Century Association. The reformation called for a return to nature. The country was unspoiled. Picnics and rambling walks were inspirational, edifying. Communities like Brook Farm and the Berkshire country houses brought one closer to nature. Houses could be comfortable but not showy. One walked to social engagements along the dark lanes accompanied by one servant engaged to carry the lamp. At dinner, one pulled back one's own chair at table. These precepts of the American Lake District were soon to disappear. (Courtesy of J. Graham Parsons.)

BONNIE BRAE, 1886. Henry A. Barcley built this New England Shingle–style home, and no style better represented the American Lake District. In size and comfort, it was a far cry from the regulation house and the early "Stagecoach Georgian." In the changing climate of New England, the shingles weathered, becoming harmonious with the natural landscape. It was a style that accomplished both goals of the earlier colony at Lenox: large, comfortable, and neither ostentatious nor standing out from the natural surroundings. The startlingly white Neoclassic structures to follow represented a different summer resident with a different philosophy and purpose for being in the country. (Courtesy of Ed Darrin.)

EDGECOMB, 1880. At times, these civilized exteriors masked and muffled the brouhaha within. Landscape gardener Ernest Bowditch could not satisfy Clementine Furness at Edgecomb. She frightened Bowditch with her shouting and confused him with contradictory instructions. He consulted her neighbor Charles Lanier, who was engrossed in problems with a contractor. J. J. Clarke had threatened to sue for payment, while Lanier's architects, Peabody & Stearns, urged Lanier to sue Clarke for shoddy work. (Courtesy of the Lee Library; photograph by E. A. Morley.)

WINDYSIDE, 1875. On July 12, 1875, John Cook sold to Richard C. Greenleaf of Boston "property on Yokun Avenue in consideration of $6000." Greenleaf built the house that he eventually sold to the Lenox Club for Gentlemen. Founded in the 1860s, the club originally stood beside Brotherhood House on Walker Street. Some scoffed at the importance of men's clubs and said, "They sat around all day playing whist and smoking cigars." The Brotherhood disappeared, but the Lenox Club adapted, offering tennis, golf, and croquet, and survived. (Courtesy of the Lee Library; photograph by E. A. Morley.)

WOODCLIFF. E. J. Woolsey and William Aspinwall of New York built on the ridge line, and on their 500 acres, they developed eight miles of "drives." It was said that from the house one could see Connecticut. Rumors constantly spread that the property would come on the market. Morris K. Jesup authorized his agent to offer $800 per acre but was unsuccessful. Woodcliff was razed, and the Aspinwall Hotel was built. (Courtesy of the Lee Library; photograph by E. A. Morley.)

THE REMAINS OF THE LITTLE RED SHANTY. Some claim the three most important desks in early American letters were in the Berkshires: where Jonathan Edwards wrote *Freedom of the Will*, where Herman Melville wrote *Moby Dick*, and where Nathaniel Hawthorne wrote *House of Seven Gables*. Melville's desk still sits in his house, the Arrowhead Museum. Edwards's house was razed; the desk is now in the Stockbridge Library. When Hawthorne's house burned in 1890, the desk was lost. (Author's collection.)

NEWTON'S PLACE ON CLIFFWOOD. The Honorable Mr. Newton held one of the important book collections in the Berkshires. His library door was open to all who wished to read, but he had a singular quirk. All elaborate covers were to be replaced with plain bindings. Local bookbinders, struck by the artistry of some ancient covers, complained. Newton was firm, saying, "I want readers attracted by the title and subject matter, not a showy binding." (Courtesy of the Lee Library; photograph by E. A. Morley.)

BREEZY CORNER. This house was built by Jonathan William and Emily Meigs Biddle of Philadelphia. The Biddles, who came to the Colonies with William Penn, were well-respected bankers and lawyers who served every president from George Washington to Franklin D. Roosevelt. George and William Biddle disappointed their family by becoming a painter and a writer, respectively. Such judgments are relative, and all must have been forgiven when the profession of Sydney Biddle Barrows, the Mayflower Madam, was revealed. The Biddles, Lippincotts, and Whartons were all related. (Courtesy of the Lee Library; photograph by E. A. Morley.)

NOWOOD, 1885. Water, and getting it to the many houses being built, was a serious problem. So, when the *Valley Gleaner* reported that R. W. Chapin at Nowood had completed his "private waterworks with a reservoir, an engine, and 1000 feet of pipe," it was not certain whether the feature was a decorative or a practical one. (Courtesy of the Lee Library; photograph by E. A. Morley.)

SUNNY RIDGE, 1884. George Winthrop Folsom began to assemble his land in 1881. Over the next 20 years, there were a dozen separate transfers of land. The result was not just a summer house; it was one of the earliest summer estates. The house, designed by architect C. C. Haight, is an American adaptation of Early English architecture. (Courtesy of the Lee Library; photograph by E. A. Morley.)

STONOVER, 1875. In 1885, the *Valley Gleaner* reported, "Mr. John E. Parsons' additions to his already sizeable mansion are approaching completion with its adjuncts of stable, lodge house, forest, field, and beautiful outlooks over lake and mountain." (Courtesy of the Lee Library; photograph by E. A. Morley.)

GUSTY GABLES. Mary DePeyster Carey and Edith Rotch, sister of architect Arthur Rotch, owned Gusty Gables. While the women were in Europe, Morris K. Jesup rented it and met there with Arthur Rotch to plan Belvoir Terrace. The architectural firm of Rotch and Tilden designed five houses in Lenox: Belvoir Terrace, Osceola, Ventfort Hall, Thistledown, and the Frelinghuysen Cottage. Both Arthur and Edith Rotch died young, she at Gusty Gables. (Courtesy of the Lee Library; photograph by E. A. Morley.)

THE FREDERICK T. FRELINGHUYSEN HOUSE. For Frederick Frelinghuysen, 1881 was a good year: Pres. Chester A. Arthur appointed him secretary of state, and his house at Lenox was completed. Rotch and Tilden designed a sophisticated blend of Georgian and Federal and then blew it completely out of scale, just as all the houses of the coming era were to be. Frelinghuysen's wife, Matilda Griswold, came from the prominent shipping family that held the China–Liverpool–New York route; his granddaughter Sarah married Henry Cabot Lodge. (Courtesy of Ed Darrin.)

BROOKHURST. Architect James Renwick designed Grace Church and St. Patrick's Cathedral in New York City, the Smithsonian Institution in Washington, D.C., and this house in Lenox. Brookhurst was built for W. B. Shattuck. The architects had arrived in Lenox, presaging the coming of the Gilded Age resort. (Courtesy of the Lee Library; photograph by E. A. Morley.)

HOMESTEAD, 1885. Charles Folsom McKim of McKim, Mead, & White designed this house for the Appleton sisters. It became a labor of love, literally. Just as Henry Wadsworth Longfellow before him, McKim fell in love with "one of the Appleton girls." He and Julia Appleton married in 1885 and honeymooned at Homestead. Longfellow and McKim were destined to have more in common: both wives died prematurely in freak household accidents. Frances Appleton Longfellow was sealing a package with hot wax when it burst into flames. Julia Appleton McKim was descending the staircase and lost her footing. It was the staircase at Homestead, the one McKim designed, of which he had been particularly proud. McKim became a widower before his first wedding anniversary. Although he returned often to the Berkshires, designing St. Paul's Church, Naumkeag, and Trinity Church, McKim never returned to Homestead. (Courtesy of the Lee Library; photograph by E. A. Morley.)

GLAD HILL. In 1888, Trinity Church was nearing completion when it was proposed that a Tiffany window be purchased to grace the church. Mrs. Philip J. Sands hosted a successful fund-raising event at Glad Hill. The window, along with many other gifts from the permanent summer residents, was installed. Edward and Edith Jones Wharton rented Glad Hill for the 1900 season. (Courtesy of the Lee Library; photograph by E. A. Morley.)

THE DORMERS. This house was built for R. T. Auchmuty and his wife, the sister of F. A. Schermerhorn. Auchmuty was a forward-thinking fellow. In 1877, he opened Sunset Terrace House—what must have been the first motel. Under the management of William D. Curtis, it was a long building of "rooms singly or en suite all connected by hall in basement and covered walkway above." Alas, it failed, an idea whose time had not yet come. (Courtesy of the Lee Library; photograph by E. A. Morley.)

WYNDHURST. In 1869, Rev. Henry Ward Beecher wrote to Gen. John F. Rathbone that he was in urgent need of money and would like to sell him Blossom Farm. The general was interested, writing that he intended to rename it Beecher Hill in honor of the minister. Rathbone then learned Beecher needed money to defend himself in a divorce case in which he had been named corespondent. The woman was a parishioner. Rathbone instead named his new property Wyndhurst. (Courtesy of the Lee Library; photograph be E. A. Morley.)

THE WYNDHURST INTERIOR. Gen. John F. Rathbone moved Beecher's Blossom Farm house aside to be used by his groundskeeper and built Wyndhurst. Considered a fine house during the Lake District period, it did not meet the standards of the next generation. Rathbone's house was moved downhill and used by the superintendent of grounds. Rathbone's fine house was considered no better than a workman's cottage in the Gilded Age. (Courtesy of the Lee Library; photograph by E. A. Morley.)

PINE CROFT. F. A. Schermerhorn's summer house was also a working farm. Although he and the entire Schermerhorn family were known and respected during their day, history remembers only one. Caroline Schermerhorn married William Blackhouse Astor. The combination of her lineage and his money established her as *the* Mrs. Astor, grande dame of New York society. (Courtesy of the Lee Library; photograph by E. A. Morley.)

HIGHLAWN, 1842. George Dorr was credited "with the best lawns in Lenox." Highlawn was much admired as a large and comfortable house, advantageously sited upon a hill. It was not however, going to serve the next wave of Berkshire visitors. The only perceived advantage was the land. Highlawn became one of three parcels combined to create the great estate of Blantyre. (Courtesy of the Lee Library; photograph by E. A. Morley.)

THE CORNERS, 1860. Anson Phelps Stokes called upon landscape architect Ernest Bowditch to solve two problems: the house was atop a hill with no water, and the drive was quite long and so narrow no coach could turn around. The sight of a coach backing down the steep hill was sad enough, but the whole affair was complicated by a "terrible neighbor" who would not allow a widening if it infringed on his land. (Courtesy of the Lee Library; photograph by E. A. Morley.)

SHADOWBROOK. That terrible neighbor was George Higginson, Ernest Bowditch's cousin—actually, an obliging fellow. He readily agreed to widen the drive, provided he could see the house plans. He feared a house too large would spoil the beauty of the hillside. Sadly, Higginson knew nothing of architectural plans. He inspected and approved them, never realizing they were plans of the largest private residence ever built in the United States excepting Biltmore. (Author's collection.)

NESTLEDOWN. In 1885, Mrs. H. T. Sloane advertised her summer house for rent at $4,000 a month. It offered 11 bedrooms, a parlor, dining room, kitchen, laundry, and bath. Outside, it had a stable with seven stalls and room for the coachman. (Courtesy of the Lee Library; photograph by E. A. Morley.)

TOWNSFOLK. A typical house cost about the same to build as the outlanders were paying to rent Nestledown. The "improvements" at Stonover cost $100,000. This disparity of income was great and growing. A local laborer was paid $1 to $1.25 per day. The telephone company was paid $1.75 for three minutes. Townsfolk were paid $2.50 per month to board a horse, the price of a suit. Land jumped from 30 shillings per 100 acres to $50 per acre and then to $1,000 for 4 acres—and it was still rising. (Author's collection.)

OLD BERKSHIRE LANE. The narrow dark lanes would be widened by the cottagers and lit by William Stanley and George Westinghouse. The lone white house at the end of the lane, offering light and warmth, victuals and flip (essentially beer and a dump, or shot of whiskey) was crowded between hotels and summer houses, dwarfed by the Berkshire cottages. Much of what had been was swept away, but the next change was monumental and indelible. (Courtesy of Lion Miles.)

THE FIRST HOME OF ZENAS CRANE. Zenas Crane lived in this house when he placed this advertisement in the *Pittsfield Sun*: "Americans! Encourage your own manufactories and they will improve. Ladies, save your RAGS." Until then, odds and ends of the family wardrobe were looked upon as useless. Now, Crane and his partners wanted every scrap. Why did these gentlemen want Grandma's old nightie? To make better paper. (Courtesy of the Crane Archives.)

THE ESTATE OF ZENAS CRANE. The Crane Paper Company was established in Dalton in 1801. The company could figure the payroll on the fingers of one hand—one engineer, one vat man, one coucher, and a general helper. A single contract can change a company's fortunes and a man's house. In 1847, Zenas Crane developed a very special paper. Linen threads were cleverly incorporated into the paper lengthwise. Thus, Granny's nightie found a new use. In 1879, the Crane Paper Company secured its most illustrious customer: the U.S. government. The paper required by our government?—the paper for our money. Crane's crafty insertion of linen threads made the paper feel more like money and made the bills harder to counterfeit. From that day to this, all the paper for every bill has been made in Berkshire County. Wherever the buck might stop, it started here. Zenas Crane's new home reflected his success. (Courtesy of the Crane Archives.)

A View of Stockbridge Bowl. Historians argue about who brought the artists to the Berkshires. Each credits his personal favorite, and each is right. Judge Theodore Sedgwick, Catharine Sedgwick, the Fields brothers, William Cullen Bryant, and the Century Association founders all contributed to the Berkshires becoming known as the American Lake District. They brought the artists, but it was the landscape that kept the artists coming back. The land, the lush beauty, did not change, but slowly those attracted to it were different. The hills and lakes did not change, but slowly the reasons for coming changed. The artists and writers gave the Berkshires panache, which attracted the wealthiest and most powerful in the land. They built their Berkshire cottages and created formal gardens, and the natural beauty became a backdrop. The era of the Lake District was over; the Gilded Age had arrived. (Author's collection.)

Three
A GILDED AGE RESORT
GREAT ESTATES

THE ORGAN AT KELLOGG TERRACE. The Gilded Age was a time when vast new wealth was disproportionately distributed into a few hands. The New York City palaces and the Newport and Berkshire cottages were the symbols of the age. Mary Kellogg (Mrs. Mark) Hopkins named her cottage in Great Barrington Kellogg Terrace, although it has also been called Searles' Castle after her second husband. (Courtesy of James E. Treat.)

KELLOGG TERRACE. A cottage was defined as a country house of no less than 20 rooms on no less than 30 acres. People called them Berkshire cottages for the same reason they called the Atlantic Ocean "the Pond": they were fans of visual display and verbal understatement. The nouveau riche spared no effort or expense to establish that they held the power and stood at the pinnacle of society. Fortunately for the arts and the fledgling professions of architecture and landscape architecture, they also spared no expense demonstrating their taste and discrimination. They have been called by many names, including the 400, the princes of industry, the barons of finance, robber barons, and the shepherds of the American Renaissance. They were called cottagers by the locals, and they had arrived. (Author's collection.)

THE JUDGE BISHOP HOUSE. Built in 1855, this home remained in the family until 1906. In 1896, Henry W. Bishop wrote, "Dear Post: New England Telephone Co. wishes to use poles on my land for the purpose of extending their lines. There seems to be a general impression that my land can be used for any purpose desired. I have declined." Lenox had become a sophisticated Gilded Age resort, and Bishop's house was at the center of new growth. (Courtesy of the Lee Library; photograph by E. A. Morley.)

SUNNY CROFT. In 1887, from Wall Street, G. G. Haven wrote attorney Thomas Post regarding the purchase of six contiguous lots, 32 acres, for $93,000. Lenox was attracting the carriage trade, and the unostentatious summer house would not do. Unfortunately, to create a cottage, a barn had to be moved at a cost of $371. Cottagers were sometimes called penny-wise and pound-foolish, as Haven wrote, "Post: send estimate to purchase another 12' to leave barn and have a path wide enough for a cart." (Author's collection.)

OSCEOLA. On October 11, 1888, the *Pittsfield Sun* reported, "Mr. Rotch, the millionaire architect of Boston, who designed the Frelinghuysen mansion, has made plans for a lovely little cottage for Mr. Edward Livingston who lately bought the Newton property. The Newton house has been sold for removal." Livingston's Osceola was a polished Georgian Revival with a piazza running the length of the house. It was judged superior to Mr. Newton's in every particular. (Courtesy of the Cliffwood Inn.)

THE BELVOIR TERRACE EXTERIOR. Morris K. Jesup retired at 54 and set about fulfilling his three wishes. The first was to build his dream house. With architects Rotch and Tilden, he constructed Belvoir Terrace. His second wish was to finance exploration, so he funded Commodore Robert Peary's expedition to the North Pole. His final wish was to create a natural history museum. With friends J. P. Morgan and Charles Lanier, he raised money and built the Museum of Natural History in New York City. (Author's collection.)

THE BELVOIR TERRACE INTERIOR. Morris K. Jesup was a hard man of business. He approached every task with the same tenacity and perspicacity. Yet, at home he was mild and loath to argue. If he wanted landscape architect Ernest Bowditch to make a change, Jesup would say, "Mrs. Jesup is unhappy." Once, Jesup used this ploy in front of Marian DeWitt Jesup. She demurred, "I never said that." He was undaunted, replying, "You know you would have said so if consulted." (Courtesy of Nancy Goldberg.)

FRELINGHUYSEN COTTAGE. A coach-and-four draws up in front of Frelinghuysen Cottage. The coach required two in help: the coachman and the footman. Here, the footman steadies the horses. (Courtesy of the Lenox Library.)

THISTLEDOWN. The entrance is Federal, reminiscent of both Frelinghuysen and Osceola. The street face is eclectic and oddly similar to Belvoir Terrace, not in the fabric of the building but in the curving wings on either side of the recessed porch. This is not surprising, as Rotch and Tilden designed Thistledown in 1890 for David and Hannah Lydig. Hannah Lydig engendered more gossip than ordinarily associated with the ladies of the cottages, but it was of a peculiar kind. (Author's collection.)

THISTLEDOWN. In life, the behavior of Hannah Lydig and neighbor F. Augustus Schermerhorn was impeccable. When Schermerhorn died in 1919, however, he left Lydig $550,000, his Lenox estate Pine Croft, and 1,400 acres. The will read, "For Hannah Minthorne Lydig my lifelong and dearest friend." The rumors flew. When Lydig died, her will raised no fewer eyebrows. There was a claim by Dr. Jesse W. Hedden for $12,000 in fees and $50,000 in other services. Lydig was, therefore, looked upon as a "hot item," 19th-century style, having had a husband, a lover, and a madcap affair with her doctor. The next occupants of Thistledown eclipsed even these rumors. Upon Lydig's death, Thistledown passed to David Lydig's brother Philip. When Philip divorced his wife, Rita de Costa Stokes, she gave up custody of her son W. E. D. Stokes for $1 million. The story of the "million-dollar baby" was front-page news. (Author's collection.)

THE GHOST IN THE GRAVEYARD. The rumors failed to mention that David Lydig named F. Augustus Schermerhorn trustee of his wife's estate, and the $550,000 may have been hers. The rumors about the doctor omitted that Hannah Lydig was 80 years old when he tended her. The doctor settled for $7,500 in fees. The Lydigs were buried side by side in the Church on the Hill Cemetery. The mist over the graveyard is seen by some as the ghost of Hannah Lydig rising above Lenox to express her displeasure. (Author's collection.)

THE HORSE SHOW, 1905. They came to enjoy themselves and impress one another. In the Gilded Age, neither "competition" nor "discrimination" was a dirty word. Residents competed at flower shows, at tennis and golf, and at the gymkhana. They raced cars and horses and carriages. They demonstrated their discrimination in clothes, cottages, and equipage. Here, cottagers gather at Highlawn for the annual horse show. (Courtesy of Anna Alexandre.)

COLDBROOKE. In 1882, architects Peabody and Stearns designed Coldbrooke for John S. Barnes. His son James described the house as large, rambling, and of no fixed style. Landscape architect Ernest Bowditch found John Barnes a difficult man, and his son obliquely agreed, "I avoided my father as much as possible which had now become a fixed habit." There were extenuating circumstances: earlier that year, the eldest Barnes child had died, and James, now the oldest, had been expelled from school. He was at home in Lenox that winter, busying himself with theatricals, bicycling, and sledding on Courthouse Hill with the carpenter's son, Bob Clifford. The hill was a dangerous slope because of the speed achieved with the steep descent and limited vision. During one run, an oxcart appeared from nowhere and a crash was imminent for the two boys. (Courtesy of the Library of Congress.)

COLDBROOKE INTERIOR. James Barnes wrote of the sledding incident, "[Bob Clifford's] quick thinking saved us. He grew up to be a clever contractor." Indeed, regardless of architect, Clifford Brothers built many of the Berkshire cottages. Barnes became a noted writer and editor. Among his friends and colleagues was another associated with sledding on Courthouse Hill: Edith Wharton (of the Mount). As a neighbor of Barnes, Wharton knew full well the perils of Berkshire sledding. It figures prominently in her novel *Ethan Frome*. (Author's collection.)

ELM COURT, 1886. Peabody and Stearns designed a Lenox house for William Douglas "W. D." and Emily Thorne Vanderbilt Sloane in 1886. Some call it the first Berkshire cottage, but if they do, it is not this earlier version they have in mind. (Courtesy of the Lee Library; photograph by E. A. Morley.)

ELM COURT, 1900. Three "additions and alterations" were carried out, in 1889, 1893, and 1899–1900. The final result was the 90-room Berkshire cottage that is representative of the Gilded Age. Using the elm tree in the previous photograph as a guide, one can clearly see the three additions on both the right and left sides of the original house. (Courtesy of William Osgood Field.)

FOUNTAINS OF ELM COURT. A number of requirements existed for a proper Berkshire cottage, not the least of which was the greenhouse (visible behind the fountain). These houses were built for entertaining, and fresh flowers were necessary to complete a well-dressed dining table and a well-furnished salon. (Courtesy of William Osgood Field.)

THE ENTRANCE COURT FOUNTAIN. In the Gilded Age, less was emphatically not more. A granddaughter of Emily Sloane was told that the fountain in the entrance court was a replica of one in Italy. Fascinated, she searched for the original while honeymooning in Rome. She found it with some difficulty because the original was only three feet high and set into an alcove. (Courtesy of Adele Emory.)

THE ELM COURT INTERIOR. The interior of Elm Court changed as often as the exterior between 1886 and 1900. This is the final incarnation of the library. For every function, there was a room—the writing room, music room, dining room, billiard room, ballroom, and salon. The formal rooms were downstairs, and the family bedrooms and sitting rooms were on the second floor. Servants' quarters were on the third floor, with the "engine" of the house (kitchens, laundry, coal cellar) in the basement. (Courtesy of William Osgood Field.)

A SOCIAL GATHERING AT ELM COURT. Cottages were built for entertaining. From left to right are the following: (first row) Louise Torrance Vanderbilt, Eliza Vanderbilt, Caroline Sterling (Mrs. Joseph) Choate, two unidentified people, Emily Thorne Vanderbilt (Mrs. W. D.) Sloane, and Joseph Hodges Choate; (second row) unidentified, W. D. Sloane, and unidentified. (Courtesy of William Osgood Field.)

EMILY THORNE VANDERBILT SLOANE. A petite woman of high energy and good humor, Emily Sloane was regimented and so was her household. She took her walk at the same time every day, and all guests at Elm Court were on time for tennis, riding, and meals. She was a leader in "the colony"; when she rode a newfangled machine (a bicycle) to the post office, others followed. (Courtesy of Adele Emory.)

ISAAC SACKETT. Cottagers were the first celebrities. Their every move was recorded, and their every fashion imitated. If Emily Sloane rode a bicycle, others followed. James Barnes of Coldbrooke possessed a Pope's bicycle "of the old high type," joining the Berkshire County Wheelman's Club. Since he was a cottager and the others were locals, he did not tell his father. Here, Isaac "Ike" Sackett, a local and member of the Wheelman's Club, sits astride his high-type bicycle. (Courtesy of Christopher Baumann.)

ISAAC AND LYDIA SACKETT. When Ike Sackett married Lydia, he traded in his wheels for this contraption, the name and design of which are mercifully lost in the mists of history, and a boathouse. The boathouse was a great success. His was the only spot on Stockbridge Bowl where boats could be rented, "the lake everywhere being owned and controlled by millionaires." (Courtesy of Christopher Baumann.)

CURLING. Curling is as difficult to explain as it is to play. There is an ice rink, like this one at Highlawn with a house in the background. Huge and heavy stones are placed on the ice. The players, in two teams, are equipped with brooms. The objectives are to move the stones and to score. One does not hit the stone with the broom, but sweeps in front of the stone, causing it to move. (Courtesy of William O. Field.)

WYNDHURST. John Sloane followed his brother W. D. (of Elm Court) to Lenox. He hired the same architects, Peabody and Stearns, and the same landscape architect, Frederick Law Olmsted, but there the similarity ended. John Sloane built a Tudor mansion of Perth Amboy brick. Every one of the thousands of bricks had to be shipped from New Jersey to the Berkshires. Elm Court was a New England Shingle–style cottage built with local materials, including white marble. (Author's collection.)

THE WYNDHURST INTERIOR. The loggia connected the music room in the main house to the billiard room on the ground floor of the tower. At the far end of the billiard room was an inglenook, and cleverly concealed on either side of the hearth were narrow staircases to the tower. John Sloane had moved Gen. John F. Rathbone's house aside because Berkshire cottages were sited for maximum views. From the tower at Wyndhurst, the view is breathtaking. (Courtesy of the Library of Congress.)

WYNDHURST. Of the 250 acres, 40 were lawn, 30 were woods, and the remainder was divided between farm and gardens. The tower is seen at the right of the photograph. For 20 years, A. J. Loveless was superintendent of grounds. He was "a heavy prize winner at exhibitions" and did "some good work in hybridization of amaryllis and orchids," according to his colleagues. (Courtesy of the Providence Library.)

THE WYNDHURST PORTE-COCHÈRE. Wyndhurst was an impressive, well-ordered, and decorative estate, except that the porte-cochère kept falling down. Peabody and Stearns tried to repair it, but the architects were forced to redesign and rebuild it. Here, John Sloane's coach-and-four is drawn up under the porte-cochère in apparent safety. (Courtesy of the Lenox Library.)

THE GARDENS AT WYNDHURST. The plantings at Wyndhurst reflect the philosophy of Frederick Law Olmsted to create natural settings. Shrubbery was massed, and lines were gently curving, with an emphasis on trees and a harmony with distant natural views. There was only one formal garden, shown here. A stable included 16 boxes, a poultry shelter, and a cow barn. Milk and cream were shipped daily to the family in New York, and produce was shipped three times a week. (Courtesy of C. D. Loveless.)

THE ELECTRIC CAR. Evelyn Sloane (Mrs. William) Griswold and her children—Ursula, Adela, Evelyn, Billy, and John—ride in an electric car, used to tour the Wyndhurst property. A similar electric car was used by Mrs. George Westinghouse at Erskine Park. (Courtesy of C. D. Loveless.)

THE WELL AND THE COPPER BEECH. The well is overhung at the right of the photograph by a tree branch. It is a branch of the copper beech planted by Pres. William McKinley when he visited Wyndhurst in 1897. On another visit he planted an oak. (Courtesy of C. D. Loveless.)

THE ENTRANCE AT EVELYN SLOANE'S WEDDING. John Sloane had three children—William (the eldest), Evelyn, and John Jr. Evelyn Sloane married William E. S. Griswold at Wyndhurst in 1907. The entrance hall was festooned with flowers on the wedding day. The greenhouses at Wyndhurst specialized in specimen plants. Among the flowers pictured may have been cattleya mossiae and campanula pyramidalis. (Courtesy of C. D. Loveless.)

THE ALTAR AT EVELYN SLOANE'S WEDDING. A. J. Loveless developed a new variety of cattleya mossiae; rather than the usual rosy purple orchid, it was pure white. Developed at Wyndhurst, it was named for Evelyn Sloane. Campanula pyramidalis were huge bellflowers. There appears to be a beautiful arrangement of white bellflowers and orchids behind the altar. (Courtesy of C. D. Loveless.)

ERSKINE PARK. The main house was a white Queen Anne with a red roof. Set at the center of green lawns and white paths, it was striking. The interior rooms included padded satin ceilings (the first instance of soundproofing), indirect electric lighting, and every modern convenience. The paths were crushed marble from local quarries. In the back was an electric generating plant that produced such abundance George Westinghouse lit the streets of Lenox. Nickola Tesla, a man described by James Barnes as more poet than scientist, developed alternating current, the basis of the Westinghouse fortune. (Courtesy of the Lenox Library; photograph by Edwin Hale Lincoln.)

THE ERSKINE PARK GROUNDS. The main house was large and well designed, but most agreed the outstanding feature of Erskine Park was the grounds. A series of paths wound between man-made water features. Marguerite Erskine (Mrs. George) Westinghouse's electric car putt-putted around the grounds. In the far back was the playhouse for the children, as big and well equipped as most houses in town. (Courtesy of the Library of Congress.)

THE ERSKINE PARK ENTRANCE. Owners of the great estates opened their grounds to townsfolk until 1904, when a local paper reported that the gates were closed. "It is a great pity, but the practice has been taken advantage of and the owners can not be blamed." No specifics were given, but the nationally distributed *Country Life* magazine had featured Berkshire cottages and encouraged all readers to "go and have a look," as if they were public places. (Author's collection.)

CROQUET AT SHADOWBROOK. Built by Anson Phelps Stokes in 1893, Shadowbrook had several designers. The first architects consulted were McKim, Mead, and White, who drew up plans. When disagreements could not be resolved, Stokes hired the firm of H. Neil Wilson. Harry Weeks, an architect in that firm, is given the credit, correctly, for finishing the job. Whether Weeks redesigned Shadowbrook or relied upon the McKim, Mead, and White plans is unclear. In his journal, however, Stokes gives all the credit for the design of Shadowbrook to his wife. (Author's collection.)

THE SHADOWBROOK ENTRANCE. Shadowbrook was set in 738 acres overlooking Lake Mahkeenac. The property was divided into the park, the woodland, and the farm. Landscape architect Ernest Bowditch, planning few formal gardens, wished to create a natural setting with riding trails curving through wildflowers, trees, and rock gardens. (Author's collection.)

THE SHADOWBROOK EXTERIOR. Circular gardens do interrupt the linear driveway at intervals near the tower and the porte-cochère. They were decorative, but, more importantly, they created the much-needed turnabout negotiated with neighbor George Higginson. The views were matchless. (Author's collection.)

THE SHADOWBROOK INTERIOR, THE MAIN FLOOR. Simply put, this 100-room mansion was the largest private residence built in the United States until Biltmore was completed in Asheville, North Carolina. There were as many jokes about its size as people to tell them. In one perennial favorite, Helen Phelps (Mrs. Anson) Stokes about to step on the boat for Europe, had momentary anxiety that the house was too small. She telegraphed her architect: "Please make each room one foot larger in each direction." (Courtesy of Olivia Hatch.)

THE SHADOWBROOK INTERIOR, THE SECOND FLOOR. In another oft-told story, a son at Harvard wired his mother at Shadowbrook, "May I bring the Class of '98 to stay this weekend?" Misunderstanding the class year for the number of guests, Mrs. Stokes wired back, "Have guests already, please bring only 50." In 1911, Shadowbrook was sold to S. P. Shotter, partner of R. W. Paterson of Blantyre. Shotter then sold to Andrew Carnegie, who fished "the Bowl" with Ike Sackett one day and with Grover Cleveland the next. (Courtesy of Olivia Hatch.)

THE VENTFORT HALL EXTERIOR. In 1891, Annie Haggerty Shaw and Clemence Haggerty Crafts sold Ventfort to Sarah Spencer Morgan, who was the daughter of Junius Spencer Morgan, founder of the J. S. Morgan Bank, and the sister of John Pierpont "J. P." Morgan. Ventfort was moved, and Ventfort Hall, an Elizabethan Revival mansion designed by Rotch and Tilden, was built on the spot. Seemingly contrasting details like the Dutch gables were typical of the Elizabethan country house, due to the influx of Dutch refugees at that time. (Author's collection.)

THE VENTFORT HALL SALON. Many interior features carry and unify the Elizabethan exterior, like a broad carved oak staircase and pendant ceiling in the great hall. The wallpaper, light colors, decorative plaster ceilings, and the basement bowling alley are atypical of an Elizabethan country house, but typical of late-19th-century Lenox cottages. (Courtesy of the Lenox Library.)

BROOKHURST, 1908. "The Georgian house is above all sincere," wrote Edith Wharton. When Newbold Morris contemplated building Brookhurst, Wharton recommended to her cousin the services of her architect, Ogden Codman. Brookhurst and the Mount have two things in common. In each case, Ogden Codman drew the original plans and Hoppin & Koen completed the work. Codman's contentious personality was the stated reason, but just as persuasive was his extravagant taste. (Courtesy of Ed Darrin.)

THE BROOKHURST INTERIOR. The credit for the exterior design likely belongs to Ogden Codman. In 1903, Francis Hoppin told an interviewer, "The architect is the general of all the forces— the supreme command." Commander or not, Hoppin did not change Codman's axial arrangement of the interior rooms radiating from the entrance hall. What credit is left to Hoppin appears to be the decoration of the interior. (Courtesy of Ed Darrin.)

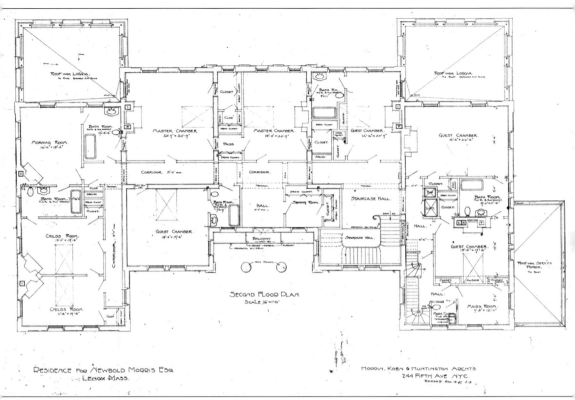

SECOND FLOOR PLAN.
SCALE ⅛"=1'-0"

RESIDENCE FOR NEWBOLD MORRIS ESQ.
LENOX MASS.

HOPPIN, KOEN & HUNTINGTON ARCHTS.
244 FIFTH AVE NYC

THE BROOKHURST FLOOR PLAN. Ogden Codman was fired in favor of the charming, fiscally conservative, and, some said, inferior architect. Francis Hoppin was known as much for his military record (he distinguished himself in the Spanish-American War), his social prowess, and his oil painting as for his architecture. Nevertheless, he was serious about his work. The New York firm of Hoppin & Koen designed a number of public buildings, the residences of Charles Lanier in New York, and the Wharton, Fahnestock, and Morris cottages in Lenox. (Courtesy of Ed Darrin.)

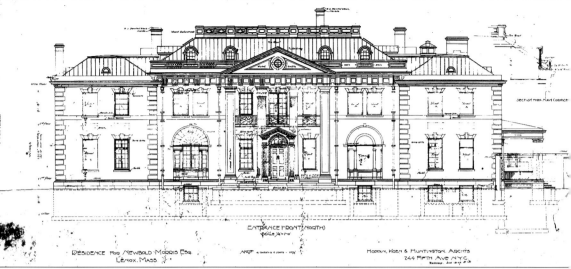

THE BROOKHURST ELEVATION. Adhering to the principles of Beaux Arts, Francis Hoppin designed house, gardens, and some furnishings. Brookhurst is a statement of Hoppin & Koen's architectural philosophy: what is functional is beautiful. According to Edith Wharton, Georgian is "sincere" because "it is a house, and pretends to be nothing else, not castle or fortress or farm." The Georgian is a large box and affords the most interior space and light without pretension. (Courtesy of Ed Darrin.)

BONNIE BRAE, STOCKBRIDGE, MASSACHUSETTS

BONNIE BRAE. Many of the Lake District summer houses were torn down, but some survived. Bonnie Brae remained in the Parsons family and was refurbished during the Gilded Age. This stationery was created by the owner for guests of the house. (Courtesy of J. Graham Parsons.)

J. GRAHAM PARSONS. The future ambassador to Laos and Sweden relaxes at home. (Courtesy of J. Graham Parsons.)

FERNBROOK. All the artists did not leave when the millionaires arrived in the late 19th century. Thomas Shields Clarke, sculptor and painter, built this cottage at Lenox in 1902. Designed by architect Wilson Eyre, it was of white stucco with a red roof. The owner called the style "Tyrolean." Clarke showed his work to advantage in the large rooms and often had "at homes," where he displayed his latest work. (Author's collection.)

CHESTERWOOD, 1901. Sculptor Daniel Chester French built Chesterwood. He selected as architect Henry Bacon, the same man who designed the bases for French's statues. French's studio was on the grounds a few paces from the house; there, he fashioned the sitting Lincoln for the Lincoln Memorial. The graceful statue in this photograph was created and placed in an alcove at St. Paul's Church by French in memory of his wife. (Photograph by the author.)

STRAWBERRY HILL. This was the home of artists Lydia Field and Rosina Emmet Sherwood and her son Pulitzer Prize–winning author Robert Sherwood. Writer Henry James, a cousin, sent annotated first editions of all his books to Strawberry Hill. Beautifully self-aware, the author of the longest sentences in English fiction said, "Don't worry, there's a verb coming." The James first editions, the Sherwood paintings, and part of Strawberry Hill went up in flames in the mid-20th century. (Courtesy of Rosamond Sherwood.)

CROWNINSHIELD'S STUDIO. Artist Frederick Crowninshield built a house and studio at Stockbridge called Konkapot Brook. On the property was a charming building that, in jest or earnest, his son Frank called his office. Frank Crowninshield was a darling of society, a man of impeccable taste and the first editor of *Vanity Fair* magazine (1914–1936). Crowninshield was first to publish Gertrude Stein, Dorothy Rothschild (Dorothy Parker), Noel Coward, and Robert Benchley. (Courtesy of the Riverbrook School.)

BLANTYRE. Robert Warden Paterson was listed in *Notable New Yorkers 1896 to 1899*. He lived at 2 West 51st Street, across from the Vanderbilts. It was a 50-year journey to Fifth Avenue from the poverty of Scotland. He immigrated to Canada with his family and struck out for New York alone as a teenager. With his first wife, Emma Downing Paterson, he had two sons, Henry A. and Robert Downing Paterson. Emma died, and in 1893, Paterson married Marie Louise Fahys. The Fahys family traced its lineage to William "the Pilgrim" Brewster, who had led the first religious service in the New World at Plymouth. In 1900, George B. Dorr (of Highlawn) conveyed "to Marie Louise Paterson certain real estate in Lenox." Between 1900 and 1904, the Patersons acquired six properties totaling more than 300 acres, retained architect Robert H. Robertson, and built Blantyre. (Courtesy of the Providence Library.)

THE BLANTYRE ART GALLERY. Robert H. Robertson was a prolific and successful New York architect. He also designed Shelburne Farm for Dr. Seward and Lila Vanderbilt Webb. At the extreme right of the photograph, The art gallery, later removed from the building, is clearly visible. (Courtesy of Robert DeLage.)

THE BLANTYRE GALLERY INTERIOR. Considering that R. W. Paterson was, for the most part, collecting contemporary art, he had exceptional taste. The paintings on the walls of the gallery are by Gainsborough, Corot, Daubigny, Diaz, Decamps, Reynolds, Turner, Millet, Morland, Homer Martin, and others. In 1900, Paterson wrote the book *Impressions of Many Lands*. One copy is inscribed to "Mr. Andrew Carnegie with Best Wishes from R. W. Paterson Dec. 25, 1900." (Courtesy of the Providence Library.)

THE BLANTYRE CONSERVATORY. There are only three places in the world named Blantyre, and all relate to David Livingstone. Livingstone was the Scottish missionary and explorer to whom Stanley said, "Dr. Livingstone, I presume?" Ann Warden Paterson, R. W. Paterson's mother, and Livingstone were first cousins. The three Blantyres are the town in Scotland where Livingstone was born, a town in Africa named to honor Dr. Livingstone, and the estate in Lenox. (Courtesy of the Providence Library.)

BELLEFONTAINE, 1897. Built for Giraud and Jane Van Nest Foster, Bellefontaine was designed by Carrere and Hastings. It was one of the most formal and impressive of the Berkshire cottages. Adults rushed to render opinions, but it is a child's view that resonates and is used here. (Author's collection.)

THE PILLARS AT BELLEFONTAINE. The Fosters had a son late in life. Named after his father, as a small child he was simply called "Boy" Foster. "I saw photos of a man and sixteen horses. He put up the marble columns on the south façade," he remembered. One man and 16 horses had raised up the columns, one at a time. (Author's collection.)

THE BELLEFONTAINE EXTERIOR. "I played in the fountain and Nanny didn't like it. I tried to fish in the water course and was surprised and disappointed when Paul the Butler told me there were no fish in it." (Courtesy of Jane Foster.)

THE BELLEFONTAINE ENTRY. "I remember Hastings, the architect. He was lovable and laughed a lot. Father ordered a lot of statues and fountains for the garden. Hastings had to place them. He didn't know where to put the last one and told a man, 'Just set it down.' It was just inside the door. There it stayed, no one ever moved it again." (Courtesy of Jane Foster.)

THE BELLEFONTAINE MAIN STAIRCASE. "There was 'Smart Fred,' the lawyer. He was so anxious to have Daddy as a client that he drank too much during the evening. He fell all the way up the stairs on his way to bed," Giraud Foster Jr. recalled. (Courtesy of Jane Foster.)

THE BELLEFONTAINE MAIN HALL. Bellefontaine was designed *en falade*, which means a hallway ran the length of the house and all rooms opened onto it from one side. The hall at Bellefontaine was created in shades of white marble, with darker marble columns and decorative marble inlay over each of the doors. (Courtesy of Jane Foster.)

THE EGYPTIAN CHAIR AT BELLEFONTAINE. Archeological digs were very popular during the Gilded Age. The pinnacle of 40 years of exploration was when the tomb of Tutankhamen was opened in 1922. Throughout the period, all things Egyptian were in vogue. Giraud Foster Jr. remembered this scene as well. "Oh yes the Egyptian chair. It was in the hall to the left of the library door. And the painting above, Daddy did hunt deer." (Courtesy of Jane Foster.)

THE LIBRARY AT BELLEFONTAINE. "This was the room most used. We didn't have a comfortable family room. This was originally the palm garden; where the men came to smoke cigars. When the third floor was added (for my nursery) the palm court was closed in and became the library," Giraud Foster Jr. recalled. (Courtesy of Jane Foster.)

THE BELLEFONTAINE DINING ROOM. "The dining room was beautiful and airy and could seat 40. The staff uniforms were very dressy at parties. The 'fourth man' [the coal man] was washed up to work the party. The head butler wore a tailcoat that was dark blue lined in red with a crest on the pocket. The rest wore black patent-leather pumps with buckles, silver britches, and vests of fine black and white stripes." (Courtesy of Jane Foster.)

THE BELLEFONTAINE LOGGIA. "This was used as the breakfast room or a place for a simple lunch. A simple meal would be melon, soup, mousse, salad, and dessert." (Courtesy of Jane Foster.)

THE BELLEFONTAINE SALON. "The head gardener, Jenkins, was an Englishman. He taught Shakespeare, was a chess champion, and organized the local cricket teams. His wife was Swedish. I loved to visit them and eat their cooking. Jenkins made miniature flower arrangements and placed them in various rooms next to the chair where Mother usually sat." (Courtesy of Jane Foster.)

BELLEFONTAINE. Giraud Foster Jr. recalled, "I came home and Paul the butler greeted me at the door. When I was small he called me 'Master Boy.' Later he called me 'Master Giraud' and then 'Mr. Giraud.' That day he greeted me as Mr. Foster; that is the moment I knew my father was dead." (Courtesy of Jane Foster.)

WHEATLEIGH, 1893. This Italianate villa was designed by Peabody and Stearns and built for H. H. Cook. It was a wedding present for Cook's daughter Georgie when she married Count Carlos DeHeredia. (Author's collection.)

THE WHEATLEIGH COURTYARD. The courtyard is hard landscape dominated by a fountain. Designer Frederick Law Olmsted was the premier landscape architect of the day. (Author's collection.)

WHEATLEIGH. Most of the Berkshire cottages were great estates with farms attached. H. H. Cook considered himself a more practical man than Frederick Olmsted. He wanted more land committed to farming (above) and livestock and less to decorative landscaping (below). Olmsted saw the opportunity for vast decorative gardens against two stunning backdrops: the mountains and the mansion. Cook prevailed by simply refusing to write more checks. Early in the project, the two parted company. (Courtesy of the Lenox Library.)

THE WHEATLEIGH GREAT HALL. Among the plans of Wheatleigh are several sketches of different fireplaces proposed for the great hall. As the focal point of a major room and the first thing a visitor saw, the fireplace was very important. This one was finally selected. (Courtesy of Wheatleigh.)

THE WHEATLEIGH GREENHOUSE INTERIOR. Two grounds men arrange an arbor over the door to the greenhouse, presumably to please the lady of the house when she visited to select flowers for the table. The great estates were labor intensive. Every morning, two to five men raked and weeded the formal gardens. Acres of lawn were mowed with hand mowers. The effect was beautiful, but every aspect of the estates was dependent upon an uninterrupted flow of cheap labor. (Courtesy of Wheatleigh.)

THE WHEATLEIGH GREENHOUSE EXTERIOR. Greenhouses were major structures on the estate, not just in size but in importance. At Wyndhurst, A. J. Loveless raised specimen plants. At Ventfort, John F. Huss, brought to this country by Frederick Law Olmsted, used the grounds and greenhouse as a teaching laboratory. At Bellefontaine, Jenkins worked all year to coax 34 varieties of chrysanthemum to bloom on Giraud Foster's birthday. At Erskine Park, E. J. Norman had "100 acres of lawn, miles of drive and powerful fountains to see to." At Elm Court, Frederick Herremans grew oranges and other fruits for the table and flowers in the greenhouses. At Wheatleigh, George H. Thompson oversaw the Italian gardens, specimen trees, vegetable gardens, and provided Georgie Cook (Mrs. Carlos) DeHeredia, a very popular hostess, with the flowers mandatory for a well-set table. (Courtesy of Wheatleigh.)

THE MOUNT, 1902. Edith Wharton wrote, "Decidedly I am a better landscape gardener than novelist." Whether or not that was true, the Pulitzer Prize–winning novelist used every part of the Mount, indoors and out, as a palate. She expressed her ideas and ideals about beauty and comfort. Wharton thought that each section of a garden should be like a room, a place to be entered and enjoyed. (Courtesy of the Edith Wharton Restoration.)

THE MOUNT. Edith Wharton called it the Mount after a residence of her great-grandfather; she also called it her first real home. As the land was a place to exercise her skills and ideas about gardening, so the house was a place to learn whether the principles she espoused in *Decoration of Houses* would translate into a home of charm, balance, proportion, and surprise. Many who visited, including Henry James, thought that it did. (Courtesy of the Edith Wharton Restoration.)

SITTING PRESIDENTS IN THE BERKSHIRES. In October 1912, William Howard Taft planted a tree at the Crane estate, Sugar Hill. In 1888, Chester Arthur laid the cornerstone at Trinity Church. In 1889, Grover Cleveland and his wife were guests of William C. Whitney, who was renting Ventfort. In 1897, William McKinley planted a tree at Wyndhurst. In 1902, Theodore Roosevelt was almost killed when his horse-and-carriage collided with a trolley car between Pittsfield and Lenox. He survived and stayed at Heaton Hall. (Courtesy of the Crane Archives.)

BOXHALL PLANTATION, 1914. The estate consisted of an English manor house, a four-car garage, a four-stall horse barn, a greenhouse, and houses for the chauffeur and superintendent of grounds. The ancillary buildings reflected the architecture of the main house. A landscape architect was employed so all would be in harmony in the immediate grounds and with the surrounding environs. (Courtesy of Lion Miles.)

BOXHALL PLANTATION. The great estates of the Berkshire were small communities with as many as 8 in help indoors and 20 on the grounds. A great estate housed the richest and poorest under one roof. The inventory of Boxhall contents demonstrates the great divide. A single rug in the family quarters was valued at $350. All furnishings in the help's dining room were worth $10. All furnishings in the three maids' rooms were valued at $48. (Courtesy of Lion Miles.)

FRANCES INNES LAWRIE WITH HER SISTER, ELIZABETH INNES. Alvah Kitteredge Lawrie, president of the Aluminum Company of America, built Boxhall in 1914, three years after marrying Frances Innes (right). The lady of the house was his second wife and had nursed the first Mrs. Lawrie during her final illness. Notions that she was a designing younger woman were soon dismissed. Two years older than her husband, she is remembered as a woman of conservative habits and a generous nature. (Courtesy of Lion Miles.)

ASHINTULLY. As its name implies, this imposing Georgian stands "on the brow of the hill." In 1910, Robb de Peyster Tytus bought three farms, 1,000 acres, to create his estate. The house had 35 rooms, 15 fireplaces, and 10 bathrooms. The Doric columns, the perfectly balanced wings, and the regiment of windows created a charming aspect. The gardens surrounding the house complemented and pleased. It was a great house among great houses, and then something happened that made Ashintully unforgettable. In 1952, it was destroyed by fire; what remained was haunting, eerie, and unique. The basement hallways, perfectly intact but uncovered, ran the length and breadth of the building. Above, the columns stood alone on a rise, huge against the Berkshire sky. For anyone coming upon it from a woodland path, the result was beautiful, haunting, and somehow reminiscent of classical architecture, perhaps the Coliseum. (Courtesy of the Trustees of Reservation.)

120

ELM TREE HOUSE AT MOUNT HOPE FARM, 1910. Col. E. Parmelee Prentice and his wife, Alta Rockefeller Prentice, purchased 1,400 acres in Williamstown and built Mount Hope Farm. Elm Tree House is a brick-and-marble Georgian with 72 rooms. The colonel's intention was to create a model farm. Prentice was a Chicago lawyer when he married the daughter of John D. Rockefeller Sr., but with the assistance of 168 in help, he succeeded in developing cattle bred for milk production in the "million-dollar cow barn." The farm raised chickens and Dorset sheep; grew apples, grains, vegetables, and flowers; kept bees; and tapped for maple syrup. (Courtesy of the Williams College Archives and Special Collections.)

COLONEL AND MRS. PRENTICE. Parmelee and Alta Prentice prepare for an outing. (Courtesy of the Williams College Archives and Special Collections.)

THE HOPE FARM CHERUB FOUNTAIN. This charming fountain was built at the center of the sunken garden at Hope Farm. (Courtesy of the Williams College Archives and Special Collections.)

HIGHLAWN HOUSE 1910. As the season drew to a close, the gentlemen of the cottages gathered at Highlawn. The footmen are in livery, the guests in boaters. (Courtesy of William Osgood Field.)

THE SHADOWBROOK BOAT RAMP. When Andrew Carnegie purchased Shadowbrook, he delighted in fishing Stockbridge Bowl. His guide from the boat was Ike Sackett, a man reputed to know all the best spots. At the end-of-season party, Sackett was among the invited guests, accompanied by his daughter, Annie. (Courtesy of Christopher Baumann.)

THE BROOKSIDE SUNKEN GARDEN. William Stanley purchased Brookside in 1904. As the main house was destroyed by fire, Stanley hired Carrere and Hastings to build a "fireproof" mansion, meaning the frame would be of steel rather than wood. The first steel-framed private home to be built was the Breakers at Newport. Across from Brookside, an Italian landscape architect created a loggia with 67 marble pillars. Thomas Page, the gardener in charge, had to wax and wrap the pillars every fall to protect them from the Berkshire winters. The pillars surrounded the sunken garden pictured here. Within four years, Stanley was bankrupt. The problem was that the wizard of electricity had once worked for Westinghouse-General Electric. GE filed lawsuit after lawsuit in a never-ending effort to claim the patent rights to Stanley's inventions. By 1908, he had lost. (Courtesy of the Library of Congress.)

A "TUB." The Tub Parade marked the end of the social season at Lenox during the Gilded Age. Small horse-drawn carts or buggies (tubs) were decorated with flowers, driven by the ladies of the cottages, and paraded through the main streets of Lenox. The parade was followed by a supper, often held at Edgecomb, the cottage of Clementine Furness. Evelyn Sloane of Wyndhurst drove the tub photographed here. (Courtesy of C. D. Loveless.)

A PITTSFIELD PARADE, 1911. A parade marked the end of the season, and a parade marked the end of an era. The boys marching off to World War I on North Street in Pittsfield marked the end of the Gilded Age. For 40 years, by contrivance of the richest families in the United States and the best architects, the Berkshires was transformed into a Gilded Age resort. World War I, followed by the Depression, followed by World War II changed the country and even our memories. The Gilded Age was over, its memory tarnished. *Country Life* magazine, which once sang the praises of the cottages on its glossy front pages, now carried advertisements for their sale at auction on the back pages. The popularity of the Berkshires rolled gently up and down like its hills—celebrated and forgotten by turns. (Courtesy of the Pittsfield Athenaeum.)

THE ELM TREE HOUSE INDOOR POOL. Many of the cottages closed during the Depression and World War II. Those cottages were boarded up and their gardens overgrown when Col. Parmelee Prentice died in 1955 and his wife, Alta, died in 1962. Elm Tree House was deserted and the indoor pool was drained when a newspaperman entered, notebook in hand. He could not resist; he sat down at the edge and dangled his feet in nothing but a memory. (Courtesy of the Williams College Archives and Special Collections.)

THE BERKSHIRES: THE 21ST CENTURY

You can still sleep in a coach inn, Lake District summer house, and Berkshire cottage.

Coach Inns
The Merrell Inn
The Red Bird Inn
The Red Lion

Berkshire cottages
Bellefontaine (Canyon Ranch)
Blantyre
Elm Court
Wheatleigh
Wyndhurst (Cranwell Resort)

Lake District Summer Houses
The Birchwood Inn
Brook Farm
The Cliffwood Inn
Garden Gables
The Kemble Inn
Seven Hills
Stonover Farm
The Walker House
The Whistler Inn

You can still visit the following:

Arrowhead
Ashintully
Bidwell House
Bonnie Brae and Eden Hill
    (at the Congregation of Marians)
Chesterwood
The Courthouse
    (the Lenox Library)

Highwood and Tanglewood
    (at the Tanglewood Music Festival)
The Mission House
The Mount
Naumkeag
The Regulation House
Ventfort Hall
The William Cullen Bryant House

My sincere apologies to any I missed and inadvertently left out. The determined visitor will find them all.

SUMMER IN THE BERKSHIRES, 1900. "Here is the ghost of a summer that lived for us."—W. E. Henley. (Courtesy of the Crane Archives.)